OMNIBUS PRESS PRESENTS THE STORY OF

BRITNEY SPEARS

Written by Ashley Adams
Cover and Book Design by Athena Aston

US ISBN: 0-8256-1744-8
UK ISBN: 0-7119-7698-8

Exclusive distributors:
Book Sales Limited
8/9 Frith Street, London
W1V 5TZ, UK

Music Sales Corporation
257 Park Avenue South
New York City, NY 10010, USA

Music Sales PTY, Ltd
120 Rothschild Avenue
Roseberry, NSW 2018
Australia

To the Music Trade only:
Music Sales Limited,
8/9 Frith Street,
London W1V 5TZ, UK

Photo Credits:
Ernie Paniccioli/Retna Limited USA: 1, 15
Steve Granitz/Retna Ltd: 3
UAZ/LFI: 4
Jen Lowery: 7, 11, 17
Anthony Cutajar/LFI USA: 8, 22
Joseph Marzullo/Retna Limited USA:12
Eddie Malluk/Retna Limited USA: 18
Steve Granitz/Retna Ltd: 21
George DeSota/LFI: 25, 30
Kelly Swift: 26
Ron Wolfson/LFI USA: 29

Front Cover Photograph: Eddie Malluk/Retna Limited USA
Back Cover Photograph: Ernie Paniccioli/Retna Limited USA

Printed in the United States of America by
Vicks Lithograph and Printing Corporation

...BABY

Just what is it about Britney Spears? She's a small-town girl-next-door with a funky, fresh new sound that has catapulted her to pop stardom. Her record-breaking debut album . . . *Baby One More Time* rocketed into the charts at Number One, and her dance-fueled video and live show has put the entertainment back into the entertainment industry and the pop back into popular music. She's the alternative to alternative, and the antidote to the post-grunge doldrums. She's living, breathing proof that not all teenagers live to pierce their lips and dive headlong into the mosh pit. Britney Spears represents talent, dedication, hard work, and squeaky-clean good fun—and there's nothing wrong with that. Just ask her hundreds of thousands of fans.

BABY

TRAMPOLINES

Nowadays, when Britney Jean Spears returns to her hometown of Kentwood, Louisiana, each and every one of its residents knows who she is. They line up to greet her holding banners saying, "We love you, Britney!" But then again, most of the tight-knit community of less than 2,500 knew her before she became famous. We're talking about a small town, and Britney has always been one to draw a bit of attention.

Ever since she was a tiny tot, the future pop star loved singing, dancing, and performing, and at an age when most girls just wanna have fun, she was determined to start a professional career. As legend has it, Britney's mother actually discovered her daughter's singing talents. "I would always drive my mom crazy, you know, singing," Britney confesses on her enhanced CD. "I'd drive her nuts." One day little Brit was jumping on her trampoline and singing away when her mother lent an ear and realized her daughter was perfectly on key. However, this is not the typical, oft-heard saga of a domineering "backstage mom" pushing her kid. Britney didn't need any pushing—she was the one who made up her mind to go for it. She knew that singing in front of the mirror with a bottle of hairspray as a microphone wasn't going to get her very far. A mere babe, she enrolled in the local Renee Donewar's School of Dance and hit the stage whenever she had the opportunity, be it the Kentwood Dairy Festival or her own kindergarten graduation ceremony. Her very first public performance was at the age of four singing "What Child Is This" at church. Gymnastic meets were another release for all of her pent-up energy, and Britney's competitive spirit and dedication paid off nearly every time. She had the taste—and the talent—for performing, and soon her small-town gigs just weren't enough. Church choir, local dance reviews, and shopping mall Christmas shows were lots of fun, but they didn't satisfy Britney, and only made her determined to move on up.

When she was just eight years old, the bright little girl auditioned for the new *Mickey Mouse Club*, which was making quite a comeback on the Disney Channel. Although Britney thought she was mature enough to take on the show, the MMC producers felt she was just a little too young. But all was not lost. Proving that it never hurts to try, Britney's failed audition turned out to be very helpful for the aspiring young entertainer. One of the show's producers saw a lot of promise there and helped Britney to hook up with an agent. This

AND TROPHIES

is how it was that Miss Spears left her little hometown to head for the big city: New York. She enrolled at the prestigious Professional Performing Arts School and the Off-Broadway Dance Center, where she honed her talents studying for the following three summers. She knew that many of her family's friends in Kentwood thought it was a just a tad outrageous to take a young girl out of the safe and sound town and make such a bold move, but Britney was confident that this was the only way to go, and her family supported her determination. "I was really thankful because my parents . . . you know most parents are the one pushing the child. I was the one, because I'm from a small town and people were like, 'You're sending your daughter to New York? Are you crazy?'" Britney said in her America Online interview. "But I was the one who wanted to do it, and I'm thankful because they were so supportive."

Most kids might not particularly fancy spending all summer long hard at work, but Britney loved it. In fact, it still wasn't enough to keep her insatiable performer's appetite satisfied. She managed to fit in some commercial work on the side to jazz things up a bit. An opportunity to further hone her acting skills came up when she secured a role in an off-Broadway show called *Ruthless* in 1991. The play was based on an old thriller called *The Bad Seed* which opened in 1956. Britney showed her mischievous nature when she later reminisced, "At ten I was playing this really bad child who seems real sweet but she's evil too. It was so much fun."

The budding young performer squeezed in a few honors during her city-slicker dance training. She was awarded the title of Miss Talent Central States when she competed in Baton Rouge—her now-signature combination of singing, dancing, and gymnastics was working even then, and her routine to "I'm a Brass Band" won the judges over. Two years later she went right to the top, winning Miss Talent USA to the tune of "There, I've Said It Again." A photograph of the future pop star with Ed McMahn was published in the local paper, the Kentwood *News*, on April 23, 1992, under the heading "Local Girl Wins National Talent Contest." The accompanying article noted that when Miss Spears was crowned Miss Talent USA she received "a beautiful tiara, a four foot trophy, a banner, flowers, and a check for $1,000." It seemed that the girl next door was on her way.

MOUSEKETEER

Finally Britney had reached the ripe old age of eleven, and was officially old enough to audition for the *Mickey Mouse Club*. Her three years of schooling and experience had definitely paid off, and she wowed the producers into offering her a spot on the show—she was the youngest member of the cast. "It was a lot of fun because I was like a baby," Britney said of her *MMC* days during her America Online interview. "I was eleven or twelve, and was the youngest one on the show, so people catered to me. Just being in Disney World alone was a lot of fun."

The *MMC* launched a few other young stars, including Golden Globe–winning *Felicity* star Keri Russell, Ryan Gosling of Nickelodeon's *Hercules*, and another aspiring musician named Christina Agulularia who is now signed with RCA and has an album coming out. It just so happened that there were also a few young men amongst the Mouseketeer cast that would play a role in Britney's future: J.C. Chasez and Justin Timberlake, who would go on to join the ranks of the hottest boy band around, 'N Sync. But we're getting ahead of our story. . .

"It was probably when I was on the *Mickey Mouse Club* that I realized that I had such a major love for music because we had concerts and we got to be in the recording studio and I was just in love with music. And that's when I realized, I wanna go for this," Britney would years later tell MTV's John Norris during his January 22, 1999, news feature on the teen pop star.

The *MMC* schedule of six months on, six months off, allowed for a fairly normal preteen lifestyle, and kept energetic, ambitious Britney satisfied. However, the show did not, as they say, go on, and Britney left Orlando to return to Kentwood when she was fourteen. For a change of pace, she thought she'd give full-time normal life a try, and attended high school like every other teenager. Of course, she just couldn't stay away from the entertainment lifestyle she had already come to love. It seemed that the young lady was addicted to performing, and her ambition was too strong for her to be content with simply going to school. As she recalls in her official website bio, "It was fun for a while but I started getting itchy to get out again and see the world. . . . I love performing more than anything and having people hear my music. I know I've had to give some stuff up to do this, but I don't miss high school . . . every weekend we'd go out and do the same thing. It's wonderful as long as you love

YEARS

what you're doing, but I'd rather be doing this!" She matter-of-factly added, "I've done the prom thing, but it's only once a year. I need to sing and I love to travel." Britney has gleaned inspiration from her ever-growing list of favorite artists. She admires Madonna's versatility and voracious appetite for change. If forced to name an all-time favorite song, she will choose the Artist Formerly Known as Prince's "Purple Rain." Mariah Carey is another female singer who Britney holds in high regard. "I love Whitney Houston, she's incredible. I totally admire her. When she sings, she really feels her music. As far as writers go, I love Diane Warren, she's an incredible writer. I love her songs," Britney volunteered during her America Online interview.

Sensing his daughter's "itchiness," Britney's father decided to lend a helping hand and got in touch with New York-based entertainment attorney Larry Rudolph. The lawyer represented quite a few musicians, including Ghostface Killah of Wu-Tang Clan and 98°, and he was willing to have a listen to some good old female pop music. He told Jamie Spears to send him some samples of Britney singing. Rudolph was able to get a one-song demo tape in the hands of Jive Records' Senior Vice President of A&R, Jeff Fenster, who liked what he heard. "She sang over an instrumental that wasn't in her key—but I heard something special. Her vocal ability and commercial appeal caught me right away," he told *Billboard* in its December 4, 1998, "Artist of the Day" feature. The strength of the demo tape landed Britney an audition at Jive, the home of the likes of R. Kelly, Tom Jones, George Benson, Samantha Fox, 2Pac, and the Backstreet Boys. Before she knew it, the fifteen year old had herself a record contract. "I came there with just some dinky little tape," Britney would later tell *Entertainment Weekly* in its March 5, 1999, issue. "When I signed I was like, 'This is too good to be true!'"

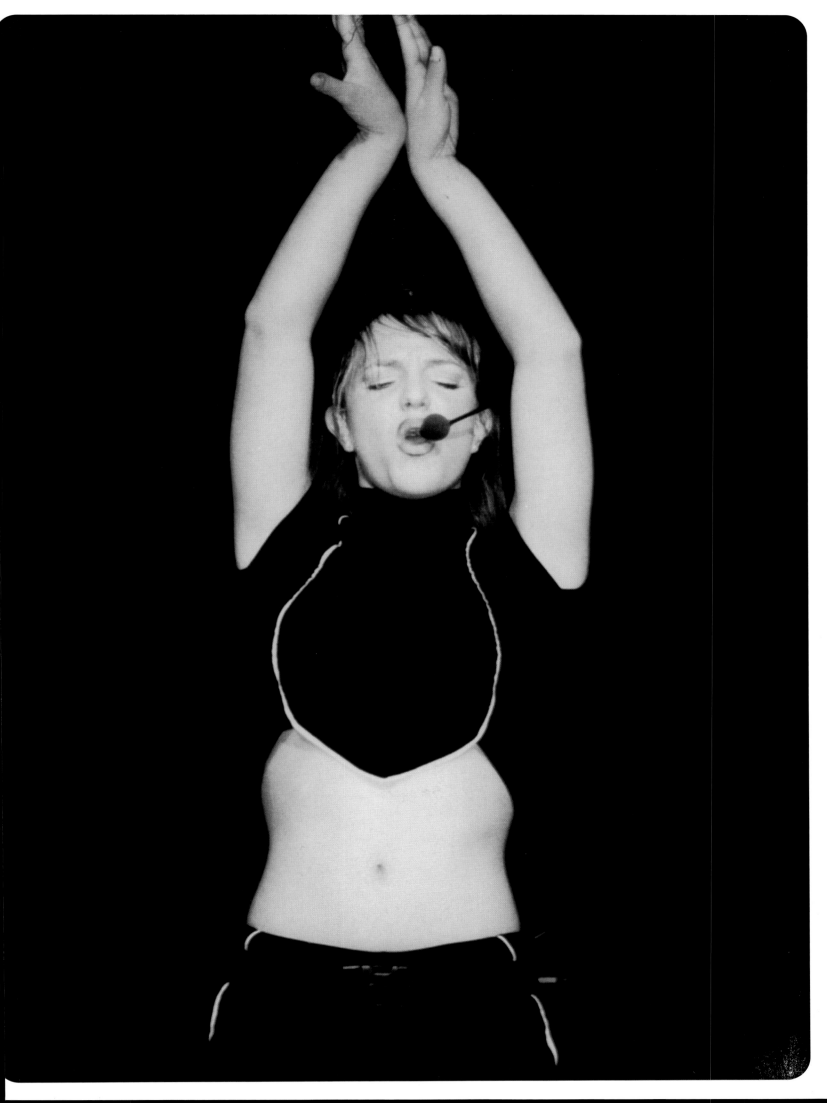

JIVE!

Too good, indeed. Before Britney knew it, she was put on a plane bound for Sweden, where she was to hook up with writer/producer extraordinaire Max Martin, whose past credits included none other than Robyn, Ace of Base, and the Backstreet Boys. The trip was Britney's first ever time abroad, but she didn't do a lot of sightseeing. Holed up in Stockholm's Cheiron Studios, Britney got down to business with a group of songwriters and musicians. The original plan to record only three songs with Martin was thrown right out the window when they all discovered how well they worked together, and the music kept flowing.

With a suitcase full of songs—including a little Martin-penned number called ". . . Baby One More Time"—Britney returned Stateside. The remaining half of the songs that would make up her debut album were recorded with yet another successful producer and writer, Eric Foster White, who had worked with the likes of Whitney Houston and Hi-Five. Wrapping up the album at 4MW East and Battery Studios, New York City, was smooth sailing.

"It was a case of good chemistry among a group of very talented people," Jeff Fenster told *Billboard.* "The writers and producers immediately saw what we at the label did: Britney is a star." Having such positive backing and support from her label certainly helped Britney take on this new challenge with her usual confidence. Jack Satter, Senior Vice President of Pop Promotion at Jive Records, was quoted in *Hit Sensations* magazine as saying, "I've been involved with a lot of different projects over the years, and with Britney, we've got a really special artist. I really feel that she's a young Madonna. Our goal is to make her into a huge pop-rhythm crossover artist. I think she's got longevity."

The marketing force at Jive Records started setting the stage for Britney's big entrance in June of 1998. Her web page, featuring interviews, song clips, and lots of photographs, was up and running all summer long. Her label sent postcards giving out a toll-free Britney hotline number to fan clubs of successful pop acts. The callers were treated to samples of Britney songs and bits of interviews. At summer's end, still months away from the release of her very first single, Britney hit the road, setting out on a twenty-eight date promotional tour cosponsored by teen magazines *Seventeen, Y.M., Teen,* and *Teen People.* Like eighties teen sensation Tiffany, she performed in shopping malls, but the similarity ended there. Britney brought her infectious sound to her audience with an irresistible set of just four songs, and gave the crowd a taste of what was to come with two back-up dancers. After whetting their appetites, Britney passed out party favors—bags containing cassette samplers of her music. Of course, performing in unconventional places can have its downfalls. Legend has it that Britney was dancing onstage at one mall and stepped on a cupcake that had made its way onstage. Her routine took a funny turn, but one of her dancers, T.J., picked both the offending dessert and Britney up off the floor and saved the day. That little mishap aside, the mini-tour was a success. As Jive's Director of Marketing, Kim Kaiman, put it in *Billboard's* December 4, 1998, "Artist of the Day" feature on Britney, "The response was tremendous. . . . Kids were intrigued by Britney. We knew that we had this great package—a gifted singer who could also dance like a dream. We knew people would go for her once they saw her."

Now that a few select crowds of kids had seen her, on October 23, 1998, a larger audience got the chance to hear her, when the Britney Spear single ". . . Baby One More Time" was released. It was an instant success. The hit is as infectious as pop music gets, but there's more to this song that a catchy hook. Britney's voice is showcased here, from its sexy, funk/soul sound to its sweet and innocent quality. With elements of Toni Braxtonesque baritone, All Saints and TLC style soul, and a church-choir-trained earnestness, Britney's singing sensibility is bang on target. The single's funky attitude adds depth—this is no one-dimensional hit that has you singing along at first and cursing the day it hit the radio within a week. This hit was here to stay.

As Britney herself would later tell MTV's John Norris, she had a gut feeling that ". . . Baby One More Time" was the one. "The first time they brought it to the record label and they played the song, I was just like, 'This song is, you know, is gonna be it.' I was so excited. And you know, I was really worried because I'd worked for a year, for so long, and I was really hoping and wanting it to do well."

SYNCOPATION

With just one single and a few promotional performances under her belt for an ounce of experience, Britney landed the opening slot of the year, setting out to wow the crowds on tour with 'N Sync. The white-hot boy band's tour kicked off in Kissimee, Florida on November 17, 1998. Hitting the stage as a virtual unknown without an album in the stores is pretty difficult, and takes a lot of confidence, but Britney was facing another, unforeseen obstacle: the audience was almost entirely made up of girls. 'N Sync-crazy, boy-crazy girls who weren't too happy to have another girl get up on stage and delay Justin, J.C., Lance, Joey, and Chris! "It hasn't always been easy opening up for these guys, since there are all girls in the audience," Britney confessed to *Billboard.* "But I am ultimately able to win them over. I have guy dancers, too—and believe me, that helps."

Britney was truly taken aback at the antics of the oh-so-loyal 'N Sync-ites. She told MTV Radio Network, "Oh my God, you should see these screaming girls. It's unreal. I mean, the things they do to see these guys is unbelievable, and I started to say, 'Well, when I was that age I would never be like that,' but I am that age. I would never dream of going through the stuff they go through for these guys. It's soooo bizarre . . . girls out in the audience are lifting their shirts up, and I'm dying. I'm like, 'Oh my goodness, I'm not believing this. This is bad.'"

It seemed that perhaps a few of those screaming girl fans were just a little jealous of Britney's proximity to their fave group of guys, and rumors started up that Miss Spears was dating 'N Sync heartthrob Justin Timberlake. Both pop stars denied the speculation, although MTV's January 21, 1999, report on the romance rumors gave Justin's fellow 'N Syncers the opportunity to have a bit of fun. "I'm actually dating Britney," Joey Fatone, Jr., jokingly claimed. "We've been together for about seven years." Lance Bass quickly joined in, saying, "I'm dating Britney and two of her dancers." The truth of the matter was that the girl and five guys were getting along like brothers and sister.

The family-style 'N Sync tour motored on after Christmas, hitting Iowa, Kansas, Texas, and gambler's mecca Las Vegas before arriving in California. The Los Angeles *Times* January 7, 1999, review of the L.A. concert described the phenomena Britney was up against as an opening act, noting, "The sound of clean-teen spirit filled the Universal Amphitheatre on Tuesday, as thousands of girls waited for what seemed like forever to see rising pop idols 'N Sync in the flesh." The reviewer gave Britney a complimentary nod, saying that her "bubbly fifteen-minute set displayed more affinity for Madonna than Annette [Funicello]." Britney was enjoying every minute of her set. "Probably just the crowd's reaction is the best feeling when you're up there," she said during her America Online interview. "Even the songs that aren't out yet, they're still screaming, and that's the best feeling in the world because they know your music. And they're screaming your name!"

Well, when in Rome . . . seeing as she was in Tinseltown, the up-and-coming pop star decided she may as well mingle with the best of them. A beautiful Britney in a white gown and a tiara appeared as a presenter at the Twenty-sixth Annual American Music Awards on January 11 in Los Angeles.

BIG TIME

The very next day . . . *Baby One More Time*, the album, was released. It entered the Billboard charts at Number One. "I never really expected it to go to Number One," Britney told *Rolling Stone* in its February 26, 1999, issue. "With the single doing so well, I was just gonna be happy if it went on the charts at, like, Number Forty-seven or something. When they called and told me, I was sleeping so I thought they meant the single went to Number One. Then they said, 'No, your album,' and I was completely overwhelmed. I called everyone."

There was no need to call everyone, because everyone, it seemed, was busy legging it to the stores to buy the album. Britney Spears made music industry history by being the only artist thus far to debut at Number One and then, incredibly, show sales gains for the next five weeks in a row.

The album offered up an irresistible assortment of pop gems, Britney-style. The reggae-flavored "Soda Pop" was so enticing it popped its way right onto the *Sabrina the Teenage Witch* soundtrack. A smattering of ballads, including one of Britney's personal favorites "From the Bottom of My Broken Heart" were there for fans to sing along to, and the album even featured a duet with Don Philip in the form of "I Will Still Love You." Lost love is most definitely a theme, and heartbreak received a modern twist in "E-mail My Heart" (*It's been hours, seems like days, since you went away / And all I do is check the screen to see if you're okay*). The lyrics never get too carried away—after all, the artist had barely turned seventeen when the album hit the shelves— and the mid-tempo sure-fire hit "Sometimes" cautions, *"But if you really want me, move slow / There's things about me you just have to know."*

There were just two tiny snags in the picture-perfect scenario of the runaway hit album. Reports of a "computer worm" virus on the first run of the enhanced CD came out. The problem was solved before it gained any steam as the virus was brushed off as harmless, and there was no mad return rush. The second little glitch came by way of criticism of an advertisement of sorts for the Backstreet Boys next album, *Millenium*. A few seconds after . . . *Baby One More Time's* final cut, a cover version of the Sonny & Cher hit "The Beat Goes On," the listener is surprised by Britney herself. "Hi, this is Britney Spears," she says, "and thank you so much for buying and listening to my first album. It means so much to me that you enjoy listening to my songs as much as I love singing them." She then goes on to introduce three short samples of all-new Backstreet Boys songs, saying, "Now I've got something very special, just for you. I'm gonna give you a private sneak preview of some new music from some labelmates of mine, the Backstreet Boys. Hit it guys!" The promo drew a bit of reproach from journalists who thought it smacked of exploitation. Britney herself was quoted in *Entertainment Weekly* as saying, "If I would've known I had a choice, I wouldn't have done it." At the end of the day, however, the Backstreet Boys don't need much help to sell albums, and most fans probably found the "hidden tracks" a bit of unexpected fun. And there's no doubting the sincerity of Britney's thank-you to the fans. She is nothing if not grateful to everyone who has helped her along the way. The album's liner notes include Britney's "Special Thanks: First, I want to thank God for the blessing of song, and my wonderful family for their love and support." Larry Rudolph gets a mention as "that great entertainment lawyer who believed in me from the start," as does Jive's Jeff Fenster "for signing me and giving me the chance to realize my dream."

Holding its own against all the bigwigs, including tourmates 'N Sync, . . . *Baby One More Time* was proving itself week after week on the charts. *Entertainment Weekly's* album review raved that Britney "sounds so soulful and Whitney-assured, it's downright scary. Was a deal cut with Satan?" *Billboard* magazine reviewed the album in its January 30 issue, branding Britney "a talent to watch" who is "blessed with a sweet voice and a wholesome, girl-next-door image."

Rolling Stone's February 4, 1999, album review wasn't quite as entranced. "While several Cherion-crafted kiddie-funk jams serve up beefy hooks, shameless schlock slowies, like 'E-Mail My Heart,' are pure spam," it said. *Time* magazine (not exactly known for its pop music section) in its December 28, 1998–January 4, 1999, issue complained, "But ultimately not enough of this album excites, involves or surprises. Like youth itself, the pleasures of this debut are fleeting." As they say, you can't please all of the people all of the time. . . .

A few inevitable, although less-than-creative, Debbie Gibson comparisons surfaced. "I think people say that just because she sang pop music and she was young," Britney reasoned to MTV's John Norris. "My music is totally different. It's edgier and you know, we're two totally different people so I

don't see why people say that." A far more satisfying likening, in Britney's mind, was to the reigning Queen of Pop herself, Madonna. "I like being compared to Madonna, because I totally respect and admire how every time she comes out, she's grown as an artist. I take that as a compliment," Britney stated in her America Online interview. The fast-expanding Britney fan base weren't comparing her to anyone—they were all-too-ready for a fresh face and voice. Britney herself was confident that her music and dance combo is "totally different from anything out there."

Proving her word, the ". . . Baby One More Time" video hit super-high rotation mode on MTV. It gave Britney-hungry fans just what they wanted. The clip was directed by Nigel Dick and shot in California at Venice High School—if the school looks at all familiar to John Travolta or Olivia Newton-John fans, there's a good explanation. It is the very same school that was known as Rydell High when the movie *Grease* was shot there. Britney rejected the original idea for the video and came up with her own concept, and she hit it right on the money. After all, what teenaged girl can't relate to wanting to burst out of boring old class and dance her way through the halls and gym right out of the building? And what teenaged boy wouldn't mind watching sultry schoolgirl Britney, student uniform in a knot above her toned stomach, shake it in the playground? As great as she may look, the Britney in the video has boy troubles. The young man she so longingly sings about is represented in the video by a hunky guy sitting on the bleachers who might look familiar to Britney fans as he is a model for teen clothing company Abercrombie & Fitch. He certainly looks familiar to Britney— he's Brad Spears, her cousin. Young Miss Spears, never one to take things for granted, was thrilled at the star treatment she received during the making of the video. "It's so cool 'cause everyone's just like, 'Do you need this, do you need that,' and I'm like, 'No, it's fine, I'm all right!'" she raved during the video shoot. "Everyone's really nice and all these people are so cool to work with, so it's been a total great experience for me. I've never had anything like this. It's a lot of fun."

Britney expressed her positive take on the whole fame thing during her America Online interview, saying, "It's really, really flattering. It's good to perform and everything, and see the audience really know your music and get into your songs. It's awesome. It's really neat."

While Britney's album was topping the charts, the 'N Sync tour came to an end with a resounding cheer. One of the very last shows was the January 16, 1999, concert in Britney's home state of Louisiana. Baton Rouge's Riverside Centroplex had more than a few of Britney's loyal friends and family in the audience, and they definitely made themselves heard as they supported their favorite local girl.

Just as Britney was winding down from the grand finale of the tour, reality bit in the form of a lawsuit filed against her and her parents by William Kahn, a producer based in Philadelphia, who was belatedly after commission money for his management services allegedly rendered a few years prior. The suit was settled out of court.

Speaking of management. . . if you've studied your music history, you know that the granddaddy of the boy bands is eighties sensation New Kids on the Block. In a strange twist of coincidence, it is that very band that started the ball rolling for two men behind 'N Sync and the Backstreet Boys' current success—Louis J. Pearlman, a businessman who became interested in the entertainment industry when the New Kids rented a private jet that belonged to him, and Johnny Wright, who learned all about artist management from the bottom up when he worked with the Kids. But what has that got to do with Britney? Well, Johnny Wright, a very hands-on type of manager, took a careful look at his 'N Sync boys' opening act, and decided he could work a little magic on her career as well. "I saw how talented Britney was," he told *Entertainment Weekly* in its March 5, 1999, issue, "but I also saw there was more development needed." Wright officially became a part of her management team in January, joining forces with Larry Rudolph. Through his past experience with chart-topping boy bands, Wright has gained an understanding of what young artists go through. As he went on to tell *Entertainment Weekly*, "Here's a girl who basically went from nowhere to number one overnight. The Backstreet Boys and 'N Sync had time to develop, to work on performing and the press before all the pressure came down. What's going on with Britney right now is she's just getting bombarded."

But Britney seemed to be handling it all very well. One of her dreams came true when she was a guest on her all-time favorite talk show. Britney chatted

LITTLE
MISFORTUNE

with the host and performed ". . . Baby One More Time" on the Rosie O'Donnell show on February 8, 1999, joining "Mystery Guest" Conan O'Brien and Priscilla Presley. Britney sang her hit single in a midriff-baring pink shirt and dark pants, hair loose and casual. A small troupe of dancers backed her up onstage in front of the live band, and the song's video was played on several screens surrounding the stage, all making for a very successful gig, and one the young star wouldn't soon forget.

Right when everything couldn't seem to be going any more smoothly for the new star, one of life's little accidents forced Britney to stop and smell the roses. During rehearsals for her sophomore video for the next slated hit, "Sometimes," Britney injured her knee while practicing a high kick. Alone when her knee dislocated, she thought she had broken her leg, but although that wasn't, happily, the case, the injury was serious enough to compel her to cancel her appearance on the *Tonight Show with Jay Leno* and fly straight home. The video shoot, which had Britney working once again with director Nigel Dick, had to be postponed. It was rumored to feature a lonely Britney sitting on a beachfront house's porch watching people playing in the waves and thinking of her ex-boyfriend.

Typically, she didn't let a little setback get her down. A cheerful Britney welcomed a camera crew into her house to film a segment for the Forty-first Annual Grammy Award pre-show. She and her bandaged knee might not be walking across the stage at the gala event, but why not get in on the fun anyway? Throwing a junk-food-fueled slumber party to watch the Grammys with a gaggle of girlfriends was just the ticket.

Britney's knee trouble not only put a hiatus on her involvement with her dizzying assent to the top, it refused to heal itself despite her new schedule of R&R. At the beginning of March she had to undergo surgery to remove cartilage from her knee at the Doctors Hospital in New Orleans, and was instructed to stay off her feet—not an easy task for Britney—for another month. She was in good hands, as her surgeon Tim Pinney was used to working with stars; he is the chief doctor for the entire New Orleans Saints football team. Britney issued a statement which read, "I want to thank my wonderful fans and all of the people who have offered their love and support during this time."

And what about love? She sings about it often enough, but what's the scoop with Britney and the opposite sex? Amazingly, it first hit Britney that she was a hit with the boys when she arrived at a New York City shoot for MTV's Total Request Live to find a horde of teenaged guys waiting to catch a glimpse of their favorite female. After all, Britney was used to being surrounded by 'N Sync's girl fans, and this was a different scene entirely. One young man even sported a T-shirt saying, "Will you go to the prom with me?"

These days Britney's music comes first. She did have a long-term boyfriend, but once her career really took off it just became impossible to maintain the relationship. As Britney told *All About You* magazine in its February 1999 issue, "We went out for two years. It just couldn't work out because I was too busy and he didn't understand and got too possessive and too jealous, and I was like, 'Leave me alone!'" "When you're traveling, you just get caught up in so much stuff and there's no time to have a relationship. I mean, I'm home, what, every six weeks, you know? Not even that, now. And it's just really hard to have a relationship and that trust thing. If he doesn't trust you, then there's nothing there and, you know, the possessiveness. You can't have that. And I'm young and I just want to have fun right now," she told MTV's John Norris. Every once in a while, Britney might give it a thought, but she quickly dismisses the notion. She's got plenty of time for all that. "I wish I could have time to have a boyfriend," Britney told *Rolling Stone* in its February 26, 1999, issue. "But, really, I don't want a boyfriend, because I hate talking on the phone. I'm not a good phone conversation person. Long distance relationships just aren't for me."

Britney may be leading the life of a superstar, but she remains amazingly grounded, and, well, normal. *Rolling Stone's* February 26, 1999, issue described her as "a high school every girl—the cheerleading class socialite who seems like she would also be the friend of every geek or nerd who crosses her path." She does her homework, studying through the University of Nebraska's home school program. She's a neat freak. She is careful when choosing her material, and has been known to turn down songs whose subject matter may be "too adult" for her at this stage in her career. She often confesses to being a very homey person, despite her restless nature and desire to see the world. When she has the chance to be at home in her Kentwood house, she savors every minute of it. The sight of her own bed in

GOES ON!

her very own room filled with her doll collection is enough to illicit a sigh of contentment. She obviously adores her family, counting her mother, Lynne, a teacher; father, Jamie, a contractor; little sister Jamie Lynn; and overprotective older brother Brian as her main support system. It may be that the combination of the two sides of Britney Spears—the sexy, talented, professional success, and the sweet-natured girl next door—are a major part of her appeal. The delightful notion that the same singing, dancing, acting, modeling sensation taking the world by storm says "Oh my goodness" an awful lot and still addresses anyone older than twenty with "Yes, sir" and "Yes, ma'am" is just too enchanting. Nice Spice, apparently, is just what we were waiting for.

So what's next for Britney? The ". . . Baby One More Time" single is now topping the charts worldwide, and the album is due to be released in every country you can imagine any minute now. She will be headlining her very own tour once her knee is back in shape. Already looking ahead to recording her next album, Britney aspires to writing some of her own music. The teenage pop star is soon to be seen modeling in a Tommy Hilfiger ad campaign. Oh, and let's not forget her other extracurricular activity—pursuing an acting career! It is rumored that Britney will appear in not one but three episodes of Columbia TriStar Television's hit series *Dawson's Creek*. Her character? "I won't play somebody mean, and I won't play myself," she told *Entertainment Weekly* in its March 5, 1999, issue. If all goes well with her guest spot—and bets are that it will—the hottest new scoop is that in 2000, Britney may have her very own television show. "What Britney's doing here is developing a relationship with the top television company for the type of series she might want to do," Larry Rudolph was quoted as confirming in the New York *Post's* March 22, 1999, issue.

But never fear, this girl wonder won't leave her fans crying "baby one more time" in vain. "I want music to always be a part of my life," Britney told MTV's John Norris. "It will always be a part of my life and I just want to grow as a person each time each album comes out. I wanna focus on my music right now and if, like, film or something comes up, I'd go for it. But music will always be my main priority."

Discography:

ALBUMS
. . . BABY ONE MORE TIME
Jive 41651, January 1999
. . . *Baby One More Time / (You Drive Me) Crazy / Sometimes / Soda Pop / Born To Make You Happy / From the Bottom of My Broken Heart / I Will Be There / I Will Still Love You / Thinkin' About You / E-mail My Heart / The Beat Goes On*

SINGLES
. . . BABY ONE MORE TIME
Jive, November 1998
. . . *Baby One More Time / Autumn Goodbye*

. . . BABY ONE MORE TIME PT. 1
Jive M125827, BMG International 52169, February 1999
UK Single
. . . *Baby One More Time (Original) /*
. . . *Baby One More Time (Sharp Vocal Mix) /*
. . . *Baby One More Time (Club Mix)*

. . . BABY ONE MORE TIME
Jive M126764
Australian single
Interactive CD featuring bio, video, photos, limited edition postcard.

COMPILATIONS/APPEARANCES
SABRINA, THE TEENAGE WITCH SOUNDTRACK
(Various Artists)
Geffen 25220, October 1998
Walk Of Life - Spice Girls / Abracadabra - Sugar Ray / Hey, Mr. DJ (Keep Playin' This Song) - Backstreet Boys / One Way Or Another - Melissa Joan Hart / Kate - Ben Folds Five / Show Me Love (Radio Edit) - Robyn / Giddy Up - 'N Sync / Slam Dunk (Da Funk) - Five / Magnet & Steel - Matthew Sweet / So I Fall Again - Phantom Planet / I Know What Boys Like - Pure Sugar / Smash - The Murmurs, Jane Wiedlin, Charlotte Caffey / Dr. Jones (Metro 7In Edit) - Aqua / Soda Pop - Britney Spears / Amnesia (Radio Remix) - Chumbawamba / Blah, Blah, Blah - The Cardigans

Britney Spears' album . . . *Baby One More Time* debuted at Number One just after her seventeenth birthday. Here is the story of how a small-town girl from Kentwood, Louisiana rocketed to the top of the pop music scene with an irresistible combination of talent and dedication.

This book features her early performing experience, including being crowned "Miss Talent USA," dance and performing arts training in New York City, starring in off-Broadway theater, and her years with the new Mickey Mouse Club. It covers how Britney landed a record deal and found herself in Sweden recording her own album while her peers were busy attending high school. With the full scoop on Britney's tour with 'N Sync and hints about her future plans, this book is a must for fans.

This book is
Unofficial & Unauthorized!

$9.95 in U.S.A.
Omnibus Press
Order No. OP 48149
US ISBN 0.8256.1744.8
UK ISBN 0.7119.7698.8

ISBN 0-8256-174

T3-BVN-263